WILDLIFE SURVIVAL LIBRARY

The Fastest Flightless Birds
THE PENGUIN

Mike Linley

GEC GARRETT EDUCATIONAL CORPORATION

Edited by Rebecca Stefoff

Text © Copyright 1992 by Garrett Educational Corporation
First published in the United States in 1992 by
Garrett Educational Corporation, 130 East Thirteenth
Street, Ada, OK 74820. Original edition published by
Boxtree Limited

Printed and bound in Italy

Library of Congress Cataloging-in-Publication Data

Linley, Mike.
    The penguin : the fastest flightless birds / Mike Linley.
        p.   cm. — (Wildlife survival library)
    Includes index.
    Summary: Introduces the physical characteristics,
    habitat, behavior, life cycle, predators, and different
    varieties of penguin.
        ISBN 1-56074-052-3
        1. Penguins—Juvenile literature.   [1. Penguins.]
    I. Title.   II. Series.
QL696.S473L57   1992
598.4'41—dc20   92–10245
                                                        CIP
                                                        AC

Thanks to the Survival Anglia picture library and the
following photographers for the use of photographs on the
pages listed:
Jen & Des Bartlett 27; Joel Bennett 23, 28, 29; Frances
Furlong 7 (top); Sylvia Harcourt 14, 20; Annie Price 5, 6, 7
(below) 10, 12, 17, 18, 19, 21, 22, 25; Rick Price 4, 8, 11,
13,15, 16, 24, 26; Alan Root 9
Jacket photographs: Rick Price

Note: Words in **boldface** type are defined in the Glossary on page 30.

Contents

The penguin body

The penguin is one of the strangest-looking birds. It has large webbed feet and a fat, rounded body. Its wings are little more than flippers, and its feathers are short and stubby, providing a covering more like the fur of a mammal rather than the plumage of a bird. The penguin has long, stiff tail feathers that act like a third foot, helping to support the bird as it rests. The penguin's beak is long and pointed, ideally suited for seizing the slippery fish and squid that it feeds on.

On land penguins waddle around on their short, stubby legs; but once in the water they can move around at great speed. The ancestors of the penguin spent so much of their time under the water hunting for food that a pair of wings simply got in the way, and so over the

Other flightless birds

There are a large number of flightless birds around the world. The largest is the ostrich, which can be found on the African plains. Although it has lost the ability to fly, it has evolved powerful legs, making it the fastest animal on two legs.

The ostrich, like the penguin, does have small wings; but the kiwis of New Zealand have lost all trace of their wings. Kiwis walk around on the forest floor using their long beaks to poke the soil for worms and insects.

A chinstrap penguin. The penguin's long, stiff tail feathers help support it when it is resting.

The long pointed beak of this king penguin is ideal for plucking fish from the sea.

course of millions of years their wings evolved to become smaller and rounded, perfect for "flying" underwater. Penguins spend most of their time at sea feeding and only come ashore in order to breed. While at sea they build up large reserves of fat in the form of a layer of blubber beneath their skin. The blubber not only keeps the penguin warm in the freezing cold, but also protects it when it comes on land as it is bounced around by the waves on the rocky shores.

Most penguin **species** are black over their back (or dorsal surface) and white on their front (or ventral surface). Their feet and beak may be black, red, orange, pink, or yellow; and several types of penguins have yellow tufts of feathers above their eyes.

Penguin variety

There are some 16 species of penguins in the world today. They vary in size from the tiny little blue penguin that stands 15 in (40 cm) high to the huge emperor penguin at 3 ft 11 in (1.2 m). In overall shape and coloration all penguins are very similar.

The emperor and its slightly smaller cousin the king penguin are the largest species of penguin. They are magnificent birds, each with a yellowish patch on either side of the head. On the king penguin, this patch is shaped like a large comma behind each eye. The gentoo, Adelie, and chinstrap penguins are smaller in size, between 2 ft–2 ft 6 in (65 and 80 cm). The chinstrap gets its name from a thin dark line that runs around its head below its beak, which looks a little like the chinstrap of a helmet. Next down in size is a group of five penguins that are all closely related. The fiordland crested, erect-crested, Snares Island, rockhopper, and macaroni penguins all have one thing in common. They all have a crest of yellow or orange feathers above each eye that lies flat against the head

Magellanic penguins are among the smaller penguins. Like the jackass penguin, they are well-known for their loud, braying call.

Rockhoppers and their relatives have distinctive, long, yellow or orange feathers above the eyes.

Right *An unusual black king penguin.*

while the bird is in the water and then springs up as the penguin dries out. The remaining six species of penguin are the jackass, Humboldt, Magellanic, Galapagos, yellow-eyed, and the tiny little blue.

Some scientists say that those macaroni penguins which have gray sides of the face and neck should be called royal penguins. This would bring the total number of penguins to 17 species alive today. Although the emperor penguin is the largest living penguin, some fossil bones have been found of a much larger species that died out millions of years ago. This species stood over 5 ft (1.5 m) high!

Occasionally some strangely-colored penguins have been reported by scientists in the field; all-white and all-black birds have both been seen. These are just accidents of nature that occur from time to time throughout the animal world.

Distribution

All the world's penguins are found in the southern hemisphere, and in particular around the colder regions of the Antarctic. Although many people think of penguins as living only around frozen seas and icebergs, this is not the case. It is true that penguins are very well adapted to live in very cold conditions—better than any other bird on earth, in fact. But, in addition to being found in the ice fields of the Antarctic, penguins are found around the coasts of many countries and islands in the southern hemisphere. They are distributed through parts of New Zealand, Australia, South America, and South Africa, and on many of the tiny, remote islands dotted around the southern oceans. One species, the Galapagos penguin, is found as far north as the Galapagos Islands, which are situated off the western coast of South America.

Penguins spend most of their time out at sea, feeding and building up their fat reserves. Many species live and breed over a large area: the gentoo, for instance, is found all around the South Pole. But the range of other penguin species is much more limited. The Snares Island penguin, for example, lives only on and around the Snares Islands, southeast of New Zealand; and the Galapagos penguin can be found only on the Galapagos Islands. The jackass penguin is found only around South

The Adelie penguin is well adapted to life in the Antarctic. Its thick coat keeps it well insulated against the cold.

Africa; and the fiordland crested penguin only on the west and southern coast of New Zealand. In many areas the ranges of different penguin species overlap and it is possible to see two or even more species of penguin living and even breeding together.

The cold waters of the southern seas are teeming with shrimp, small fish, and squid, which are the principle foods of the penguins. It's possible to see penguins in almost any part of these oceans, often many, many miles from land. While at sea, penguins are very shy and dive underwater if ships come too close. It is very difficult to tell one penguin species from another when they are in the water; on land, though, the differences become more obvious. Once ashore, penguins are not so shy and allow people to approach very close.

Galapagos penguins live right on the equator on the volcanic Galapagos Islands.

Penguins on the equator

It may seem surprising that a bird that is so well adapted to life in cold water can be found living and breeding in the Galapagos Islands right on the equator. The Galapagos penguin shares its habitat with tropical crabs and marine iguanas, but the birds can survive here because of the cold Humboldt current, which flows past the islands from the cold seas further south. The Galapagos penguin is quite at home both in the cold water offshore and on the hot, volcanic islands.

Keeping warm

Penguins are better adapted to living in cold conditions than any other birds on earth—and most mammals, too. They spend months on end swimming in the icy waters of the southern oceans. The emperor penguin actually chooses the coldest time of year to come ashore to breed in temperatures that can fall as low as −60°C. But penguins are superbly adapted to survive in freezing conditions. Their bodies are short and rounded, which prevents them from losing too much heat. They're almost unique in the bird world in having a thick layer of blubber beneath their skin. Blubber is a dense type of fat that acts as a reserve of food; it is also a very good **insulator**, helping to keep in the bird's body heat.

Penguins have specialized feathers to keep them warm. Their feathers are short and hollow, and very densely packed. In the water the

Large king penguin chicks. All penguin chicks grow thick, fluffy, down feathers that keep them warm in the early weeks of life.

An Adelie penguin, incubating its egg on its snowy nest, puffs out its feathers to help keep it warm.

feathers give the penguin a sleek covering which helps it to swim very quickly. On land the penguin can fluff out its feathers to help keep out the cold.

Although penguins are covered in thick blubber and dense feathers, their feet are completely naked. There's nothing between the bare soles of their feet and the hard, solid ice. To prevent a penguin from losing too much heat through its feet, very little blood travels to its feet through blood vessels that are very thin; in this way very little of the penguin's warm blood comes too close to the cold outside world.

Feathers

We have seen how the penguin's feathers are specially adapted to keep the bird warm; and many other birds have feathers that are adapted for other purposes. The feathers of most birds are, of course, specially shaped to enable them to fly. Some birds have elaborate, brightly colored feathers that help them find a mate or defend a territory: the peacock and the birds of paradise are good examples of these. The sand grouse has very special feathers on its chest. They are hollow and soak up water, enabling the bird to carry water from desert waterholes to its thirsty chicks.

Penguins on land

Anyone who has seen a penguin waddling along will realize at once that they are not particularly well adapted to life on land. They walk upright with their flippers held out to either side. They have very short legs and their body skin goes all the way down to their feet. As they walk, they look a little like a clown trying to move with his trousers around his ankles: it becomes even more difficult when they try to run! In spite of this, penguins do manage to cover large distances over land. Their breeding grounds, in fact, are often some distance from the sea. Penguin

A group of king penguins: many penguins have to travel long distances to their breeding grounds.

These Adelie penguins have found that "tobogganing" makes travelling over ice a little quicker and easier.

footprints have even been found by explorers travelling to the South Pole, hundreds of miles from the nearest sea. Exactly where the penguin was going, no one seems to know.

Every year millions of Adelie penguins make their way on foot across the ice to their traditional breeding grounds in Antarctica. It's a journey that takes several days, and it may be several weeks before they return to the sea. They cannot, of course, feed during this time, and so they have to survive on the stores of body fat that they have built up in preparation for their long journey. Penguins like the Adelie, which have to travel over large areas of snow and ice in order to reach their breeding grounds, have developed another means of locomotion. They lie face down on the snow and push themselves forward using their flippers and feet, skimming over the surface. This is known as tobogganing, and it is a very good way of covering long distances quickly without using a lot of energy.

13

Penguins in water

Although penguins are very clumsy and even comical on land, they are very much at home in the water. They can travel under the waves at great speed because of their sleek feathers and streamlined bodies. Penguins appear to fly through the water: they use their flipper-shaped wings to power themselves forward, while their webbed feet make all the fine adjustments like the tail fin of an airplane. They really come into their own when chasing a shoal of fish, darting from side to side and dashing forward. Few fish can escape them.

Penguins travel to great depths in search of food. Emperor penguins, for instance, have been fitted with depth gauges and released to hunt for prey. It has been found that they will dive to over 275 yd (250 m) in search of fish, squid, and **krill**. The pressure at these depths would kill many other types of diving birds or mammals. Penguins normally only spend a minute or two at these depths, but just how they avoid getting "the bends"—a sickness caused by the build-up of nitrogen in the blood—remains a mystery.

Before entering the water to search for food, penguins carefully scan the waves for predators such as leopard seals or killer whales. If

Two Galapagos penguins take a dip. In the sea, penguins are fast and agile.

they think it is safe, they "belly flop" into the water and dive beneath the waves. If they travel over some distance, they can save energy by "porpoising" along the surface—that is, alternately leaping out and diving back into the water, just like porpoises and dolphins do. As air is easier to travel through than water, they don't use up so much energy this way. They will use this technique also when trying to escape from predators, in the hope that their leaping out and diving back into the water will confuse their attackers.

Penguins that come ashore on sandy beaches have an easy time of it, but those that live on ice floes or on rocky shores have more of a problem. Getting into the water is easy—getting out is more difficult. To overcome this they build up their speed below water to such an extent that they can emerge from the surface like a rocket to a height of around 9 ft (3 m). They emerge from the sea bolt upright

and land on the rocks or ice on both feet, with a thud, and then waddle off. Some people have claimed that penguins can reach 22 mph (36 kph) while swimming, making them the fastest birds in water; and these sudden rocket-bursts may even mean that they challenge the ostrich, which can run at 28 mph (45 kph), for the title of "fastest flightless bird". For a bird which looks so strange on land, that's quite an achievement.

Right *An Adelie penguin rockets out of the sea, and will land on its feet on the ice.*

Adelie penguins "porpoising" travel at great speed by swimming alternately over and under the water.

Food and feeding

One of the reasons why the penguin has been so successful and has, until recently, lived in such huge colonies is the abundance of its food source. In the cold waters around the Antarctic region, algae grows in the water and even beneath the ice. This is eaten by tiny marine animals called plankton, which are then devoured by the krill. These tiny shrimp roam the southern oceans in such huge quantities that it would be impossible to estimate their numbers. It has been estimated that the krill are at the bottom of a food chain that supports, directly or indirectly, over 12 million tons of warm-blooded predators. These would include penguins and other sea birds, seals, dolphins, and whales. The krill are either eaten directly by the penguins, or are eaten by fish which are then eaten by the penguins. As well as krill and fish, penguins also eat large numbers of squid (a relative of the octopus). These too gather in large shoals, especially during the breeding season.

Penguins hunt underwater by sight. Once the bird has selected its prey within a shoal, it will pursue it using its great speed and agility to bring it close enough to its prey to enable it to seize it in its beak. Both fish and squid are very slippery, and although the penguin's

Beaks

Bird beaks and bills come in a whole variety of shapes and sizes, and each one has been developed for a particular type of food or way of feeding. They range from the tiny, tweezer-like beak of the flycatcher, for nipping flies out of the air, to the huge clapping beak of the spoonbill, which scoops up sticklebacks in muddy water. Some beaks are highly specialized, such as that of the hummingbird, whose beak is very long, thin, and curved for reaching right inside flowers to lick up nectar. Others are more general, such as those of the birds of prey, and are used for ripping and tearing at flesh.

Left *A penguin's tongue is covered with rough, fleshy spines to help it to keep a grip on fish.*

A king penguin feeds its chick on part-digested food stored in its crop.

beak is strong and sharp, it is often not enough to keep a tight grip on its food. To improve its grip on its slippery food, the penguin's tongue is covered with rough, fleshy spines.

Penguins can swallow their prey both underwater and on the surface. But not all prey is swallowed completely. Penguins can store food in their crop, a sort of pouch between the mouth and stomach. When the birds have chicks to feed, they carry fish and other food to them inside this pouch.

Life in a colony

Penguins spend most of the year hunting for food and resting on the ice floes or remote beaches. But once a year they gather in order to breed. Penguins nest in colonies, or rookeries, which are usually used by the same birds year after year. Chicks reared in a breeding colony will usually return to the rookery where they were born in order to breed. Penguins breed in groups like this for two reasons: to keep warm, and to try to avoid being eaten by predators. During really cold weather the penguins may huddle together in tight bunches. The emperor penguin, which breeds in the coldest conditions, may huddle together in groups of up to 6,000 birds with as

Rockhoppers have to climb steep cliffs in order to reach their breeding colony.

The persistent penguin

The rockhopper penguin breeds on many of the islands around Antarctica, such as the Falklands. Many of these are surrounded by steep, rocky shores and cliffs. The penguins have to leap out of the water onto these rocks often amid huge, crashing waves. They get bounced around, but as they are so solidly built and well-padded they rarely get hurt. Once ashore the rockhoppers begin their long climb up the cliffs to their nesting sites. They follow paths that millions of others have used before them, using their sharp claws to grip the wet, slippery slopes. These paths have been used so much over the course of time that they have deep grooves in them where penguins' claws have scratched away at the hard rock.

This large colony of king penguins may contain many thousands of birds.

many as ten birds to every square yard. This is a tight squeeze, as the emperor is one of the largest sea birds. Each one weighs around 55 lb (25 kg). It's not just the adults that huddle together within the colony; the chicks too, protected by their fluffy down feathers, are often rounded up by their parents into tight bunches to keep them warm.

On land adult penguins have few predators; they face greater threats in the sea in the form of leopard seals and killer whales. But within the rookeries the unhatched eggs and chicks face a much greater threat. Petrels, skuas, and gulls patrol overhead keeping a sharp eye open for unattended eggs and chicks. Nesting with several thousand neighbors means that predators are quickly spotted. Should predatory birds land within the colony they are quickly chased off by the penguins. As they

run after their attackers, the penguins flap their tiny wings as though they wanted to take off after them; and if they catch up with one, which they very rarely do, they can give a painful peck with that very sharp beak.

Life within a penguin colony is not without its dangers. Penguins inside the rookery have their own particular space or **territory** around the area they are nesting in. Should the neighbors stray a little too close, they are quickly driven off with a sharp peck. Penguins go to great lengths in order to find a safe place to breed. The emperor penguin may travel more than 60 miles (100 km) across the ice to reach its rookery, and the rockhopper has to scale sheer cliffs in order to breed on clifftops above.

19

Courtship and mating

The first penguins to arrive at the rookery are the males. They set up small territories and nest sites ready for the arrival of the females. A male will continually have to defend his territory against his rivals, and fighting is common throughout the colony. Some of the colonies may contain over a million birds, and they can soon become very noisy, with scuffles breaking out all over the place. In order to avoid too much bloodshed, penguins will display to their neighbors to lay claim to a patch of land: they raise their heads and flap their tiny wings. They may even call too, but the penguin's song certainly does not compare with the melodious tune of the nightingale. At best it is just a series of honks. Its purpose is to announce that a male has a territory and that he is now looking for a mate to share it with.

The male penguin's courtship display to the female usually consists of the bird bowing its head low or raising its neck up, throwing its head right back, and waving its wings. Those types of penguins that have long head feathers will raise them up so they stand on end. In most species of penguin the males and females look exactly the same, so these displays may help the females pick out the males within the rookery. The females wander round the colony watching the displays. Eventually they pick out a mate. In some species the females very often pick out their mate from previous years. The female will then help her chosen mate fight off rival penguins from the nesting territory. One of the pair will have to remain at the nest site at all times or else it will soon be taken over by another pair.

A Galapagos penguin calls for a mate. Only this species of penguin can breed at any time of the year.

Opposite *A pair of king penguins perform their courtship display.*

20

Good neighbors

Rookeries are frantically busy places where penguins are constantly bickering with each other in defense of their territories. The exception to this is the breeding colonies of the emperor penguin. Their rookeries are surprisingly quiet places in spite of the huge numbers gathered there (often as many as 6,000 birds). This is probably because they have to rely on each other so much in order to survive.

Adult emperors waddle out onto the ice to breed during the freezing Antarctic winter when temperatures regularly fall below −40°C and often reach as low as −60°C. The land is in almost constant darkness, for the sun scarcely rises above the horizon at this time of year. Once she has found a mate, a female emperor will lay a single egg. It is then the job of the male to incubate the egg while the female makes the long trek back to the sea to feed. During the next two months the male will hardly move more than a few yards from the egg. The males huddle together very tightly in an effort to keep warm. Often as many as ten males are squashed together in a square yard. In these conditions it is essential that the emperor gets along with its neighbors and does not squabble with them all the time. Emperors do not have a particular nest site, but they do occasionally perform some small displays to each other.

Nest building

Once a territory has been set up and is owned by a pair of penguins, they have to set about building some sort of nest. Penguins have to use whatever is nearby to make a nest; because they cannot fly, they are not able to bring in nesting material from elsewhere.

Adelie penguins use pebbles to form a nest, but these are in short supply in Antarctica's frozen wastes. It is far easier for a penguin to steal its neighbor's pebbles than to search for its own: it will sneak up while its neighbor's back is turned, pick up a stone, and quickly hurry back to its nest.

Not all penguins use pebbles to build a nest. Gentoos nest amid vegetation on clifftops. They usually scrape together a mound of earth and lay their two eggs on top. Several species nest in caves or crevices, and use twigs, leaves and even seaweed to line the nest. The yellow-eyed penguin makes a nest of twigs and grass, but this is nowhere near as grand as the one made by the Snares Island penguin, which builds quite a large nest of sticks and twigs lined with leaves. Some types of penguins, like the jackass, dig out burrows on the sandy beaches where they live. Inside the burrow is a nest chamber, and the nest is lined with leaves, seaweed, and twigs.

There are two species of penguin, the emperor and the king penguin, that do not make any sort of nest. They incubate their single egg on top of their feet and underneath a special fold of skin. The adult birds cannot afford to expose the egg for a second because the icy conditions would kill the chick inside, so they waddle around with their precious cargo very carefully. All other penguins lay two eggs (the macaroni sometimes three), but trying to balance two eggs on top of its feet would prove too much for the adult king and emperor, which is why they both lay one egg only.

Both male and female penguins **incubate** the eggs, taking turns to protect the eggs and keep them warm. A penguin may sit on its eggs for several days, sometimes weeks, before its mate arrives to take over. During this time the bird cannot feed and has to rely on its

Rockhopper penguin chicks on a nest-mound made out of mud.

Opposite *Gentoos and Adelies nest on piles of stones that they steal from their neighbors.*

fat reserves to sustain it. The male emperor penguin may stand with its egg on its feet for up to two months; during this time it may lose half of its body weight waiting for the female to return from her long trek to the sea.

The incubation period—that is, the time between the egg being laid and the egg hatching—varies between species from just over a month in the gentoo to around two months in the emperor.

Raising the chicks

A penguin chick may take two, or even three, days to chip its way out of the egg. When it eventually emerges it is covered in fluffy down feathers that help keep it warm. An emperor penguin chick will have less of a covering, because it is incubated inside the body fold of its parent. Penguin chicks look very comical at first. They have an enormous stomach and huge feet.

After hatching, the chicks are **brooded** by one or other parent non-stop until they are too big to be sat on and covered, by which time they are normally able to keep warm on their own. It's when the chicks are this small that they are at the greatest risk of being attacked by predators such as gulls and skuas. This period of the penguin chick being carefully looked after by its parents may last up to three weeks; while one parent is minding the chick, the other is out at sea catching fish, squid, and krill on which to feed it.

In most species the job of feeding the young is shared equally between both male and female adult; but for some types, such as the rockhopper and macaroni penguins, it is the male who stays with the chick while his mate goes backward and forward, to and from the sea, for food. Keeping their chicks well fed is a full-time job for the adult penguins. This isn't so bad for those species that nest close to the sea, where there's a plentiful supply of food.

Three-day-old gentoo chicks. While this small, young penguins may fall prey to skuas or other predators.

A macaroni penguin feeds its chick. Penguin chicks are fed on a diet of fish and squid.

But those that nest far inland, like the emperors, have to make the long trek many, many times.

The rate of growth of the chicks varies from species to species. As they get bigger the chicks collect into small groups called creches. By huddling together they keep warm and avoid being picked off by predators. The adults are able to recognize their own chick or chicks by a combination of both sight and sound. The chicks all make slightly different noises. The chicks may move away from the creche as they get bigger and more adventurous.

Gradually the chicks lose their fluffy down feathers, and seven weeks after hatching they look much more like a penguin. Now they are ready to take their first plunge into the icy water and to feed themselves.

At the end of the breeding season the adults too shed their old plumage, which has grown very messy after seven weeks in the rookery. Once it has its new feathers, the adult returns to the sea; and the whole cycle will be repeated again next year.

A slow breeder

An exception to the annual seven-week breeding cycle of the penguin is that of the king penguin. Many kings lay their eggs in December, during the Antarctic summer. These hatch around the end of February and the chicks are fed by their parents throughout the winter. The chicks are not fully grown until the start of the following summer, some nine months later. Adult king penguins therefore cannot breed every year, but only twice every three years.

Predators

Adult penguins have very few predators. Most of those that they *do* have live in the oceans—the killer whale and the leopard seal, for example. Penguins are always very wary about entering the sea if there are predators about, and as soon as any danger threatens they head for shore. Healthy penguins are often too fast and agile underwater to allow themselves to be caught. As they are being pursued, the birds porpoise along the surface in an attempt to confuse their attackers. Underwater, they spread out in all directions, ducking and weaving, until they reach the safety of the shore. Those penguins that do get caught are either slow, old adults that are near the end of their natural lives, or young inexperienced birds that have only just begun to explore the ocean world.

A successful leopard seal will often play with its catch for a while. It may toss the penguin high in the air, thereby stunning the bird. This activity may also assist in the skinning of the penguin, as the seals sometimes find the bird's skin and coarse feathers difficult to swallow.

In warmer parts of their range penguins are sometimes eaten by sharks—especially around the coast of South Africa. The colonies of jackass penguins that breed around these

The leopard seal moves too slowly on land to present a threat to these chinstrap penguins.

shores are also occasionally eaten by lions that live along the coast of Namibia.

Although a healthy adult penguin is relatively safe, the unhatched eggs and chicks face many more dangers. These are eaten by a whole range of animals and birds. In New Zealand, ferrets, introduced by man, may eat the young of the yellow-eyed penguins. Dogs, too, may also feed on the birds in the penguin rookeries.

The chicks' natural enemies include sea birds such as skuas, sheathbills, gulls, and giant petrels. These birds patrol the rookeries looking for unattended eggs and chicks. If they spot any, in they swoop. They will eat their captured prey on the ground or they may carry it off to avoid the sharp beaks of the adult penguins.

The little blue penguin of Australia has many other predators, including falcons, eagles, snakes, and even rats. It tends to nest in burrows to try to avoid them.

Predators have very little effect on overall penguin numbers. By far the biggest threat to penguins comes from human beings.

Jackass penguins nest amid a colony of gannets as an added protection against predators.

Penguins and humans

Ever since they were first discovered by Europeans at the very end of the fifteenth century, penguins have been exploited by humans. At first the birds had never seen a human and so had no fear of them: they allowed people to approach them, and literally pick them up and carry them away. Once penguins grew more cautious, people began to hunt them. Their skin was used to make things, their flesh was eaten, and even their blubber was boiled down to form a rich oil. Their eggs, too, which are said to have a fishy flavor, were collected in large numbers. As penguins eat large numbers of shrimp in their diet, their eggs have dark orange, or even red, yolks, which made them very popular.

Although penguin hunting and the collection of their eggs has all but ceased now, their droppings are still collected in some places. Penguin dung is a very useful and rich fertilizer. Guano is the name given to the dried droppings of all sea birds. In some places it has built up over the centuries to form a layer several yards thick. Even where sea birds have not bred for many years, their old breeding colonies are still marked by their guano.

Guano collection has provided a good income for many people all over the world. Much of the guano formed around Antarctica and the southern oceans was produced by penguins. In some places, as the diggers removed the guano, they came across unhatched

Penguins, like these king penguins, were once hunted for their oil, particularly during the nineteenth century.

28

penguin eggs far below the guano's surface that had been laid over 10,000 years before! Guano collection has little effect on the colonies if it is done outside the breeding season.

Penguins today do, however, face a far greater threat from the human race. Pollution in the form of oil slicks and bits of plastic and styrofoam has already reached remote Antarctic shores, and penguins stained with oil have often been seen. The more humans explore this region, the more likely it is that there will be some sort of accident that could prove disastrous for the penguins.

Macaroni penguins. The penguin's trusting nature made it easy prey for early hunters.

In addition to polluting the penguins' habitat, humans are also beginning to compete with them for their food source. People are beginning to exploit the rich fisheries of Antarctica. Fish, squid, and even the krill are already being caught in large quantities—and the fishermen would like to take more. Unless more is done to protect the penguins' feeding grounds, they will find it increasingly difficult to survive.

Glossary

Adapted The way in which an animal has changed to suit its habitat.

Blubber A layer of fat beneath the skin.

Brooded To sit on chicks to keep them safe and warm.

Equator An imaginary line that runs around the middle of the earth.

Evolution The slow process by which animals change over millions of years.

Habitat The natural home of any plant or animal.

Incubate To encourage eggs to hatch by sitting on them.

Insulator A layer of substance that keeps the warmth in and the cold out.

Krill A group of shrimp-like creatures.

Locomotion A means of moving around from place to place.

Marine Living in the sea.

Predator An animal that hunts and kills other animals for food.

Prey Animals that are eaten by other animals.

Range Area over which an animal species can be found.

Southern hemisphere The half of the world below the equator.

Species A particular type or variety of animal or plant.

Territory An area that an animal regards as its own, where it feeds or breeds, and that it defends against others.

Index

The entries in **bold** are illustrations.